PARK CHURCH COOK BOOK

ISSUED BY THE LADIES
OF THE PARK CHURCH
ELMIRA, NEW YORK : : :

1906

Restored and reprinted by
New York History Review
Elmira, New York 2021

The Park Church Souvenir Cookbook of 1906
By The Church Ladies of The Park Church
Restored and reprinted by New York History Review, 2021
Elmira, New York

Copyright © 2021 Reprinted by New York History Review. Notice of Rights. Some rights reserved. No part of this book may be reproduced or transmitted in any form by any means, electronic, mechanical, photocopying, recording, or otherwise, without the prior permission of the publisher.

For information on getting permission for reprints and excerpts, contact us through our website:
www.NewYorkHistoryReview.com

ISBN: 978-1-950822-16-4

First edition
Printed in the United States of America

Original cover drawing by George W. Waters, artist of Elmira, New York.

For J.D.

*who asked what kind of food
Mark Twain ate when he was
in Elmira.
- Probably this kind.*

Reverend Thomas K. Beecher
1824-1900

Contents

Soups..............................3
Fish................................5
Meats.............................9
Vegetables....................11
Salads...........................13
Breads..........................17
Puddings......................21
Jellies............................23
Pies...............................28
Cakes and Cookies........31
Miscellaneous................41
Preserves......................43
Pickles..........................44
Candies........................47

Julia Jones Beecher
1826-1905

RECIPE FOR A HAPPY DAY

"Take a little dash of cold water,
A little leaven of prayer,
A little bit of sunshine gold
Dissolved in morning air.

"Add to your meal some merriment,
Add thought for kith and kin;
And then, as a prime ingredient,
Plenty of work thrown in.

"Flavor it all with essence of love,
And a little dash of play.
Let the dear old Book, and a glance above,
Complete the well spent day."

SOUPS

CREAM OF TOMATO SOUP.

One and one-fourth cup tomatoes, 2 tablespoonfuls flour, ⅛ teaspoonful soda, 1 small teaspoonful salt, 2 tablespoonfuls butter, white pepper. Stew the tomatoes slowly 15 minutes, strain, and add soda while hot; make a white sauce of the butter, flour and milk and add the tomato juice. Serve immediately.

Mrs. H. M. Clarke.

ALMOND SOUP.

One pint chicken stock, 1 pint milk, 1½ tablespoonfuls flour, 1½ tablespoonfuls butter, salt and pepper, 24 almonds, blanched and chopped and cooked in stock about 15 minutes. Then add milk and stir all together.

Mrs. Daniel E. Rice.

POTATO SOUP.

One quart of milk, 1 head of celery, 1 onion; boil together 30 minutes. Boil ½ dozen potatoes, mash them; add milk with celery and onion strained out; season with salt and pepper. One cup of whipped cream added just before serving.

Mrs. Herbert C. Way.

SQUASH SOUP.

Three-fourths cup of cooked squash, 1 quart of milk, 1 slice of onion, 2 tablespoonfuls of butter, 3 tablespoonfuls of flour, 1 teaspoonful of salt, little pepper, ¼ teaspoonful of celery salt. Rub squash through a sieve before measuring. Scald the milk with onion; remove onion and add milk to squash; season.

Mrs. S. T. Benjamin.

CREAM OF CELERY SOUP.

One pint of milk, one tablesponful of flour, one of butter, one head of celery, one large slice of onion and small piece of mace. Boil celery in pint of water from 35 to 45 minutes; boil mace, onion and milk together. Mix flour with 2 tablespoonfuls of cold milk and add to the boiling milk. Cook 10 minutes.

Mash celery in the water in which it has been cooked and stir into boiling milk. Add butter, and season with salt and pepper to taste. Strain and serve immediately. A cup of whipped cream added when soup is in tureen is an improvement.

Mrs. Ella A. Up de Graff.

CLAM SOUP.

Chop ½ dozen small clams. Heat 1 pint of milk and when it boils add the clams and half a pint of clam juice, a bit of celery, 1 slice of onion, a little paprika and one teaspoonful of cracker crumbs reduced to powdery fineness. Cook very gently for 5 minutes, then remove celery, onion and scum that has formed on top. Increase heat slightly so as to bring soup just to point where it begins to boil. Serve.

Edith Glines.

TAPIOCA SOUP.

Clear and free from fat a good, strong veal stock. Boil with this ½ cup of pearl tapioca (that has been cooked over night) for one hour. Just before serving add, and heat thoroughly, 2 cups of good cream. Season to taste.

Mrs. Fred A. Hudson.

IMITATION MOCK TURTLE SOUP.

One pint black beans, 2 quarts cold water, 2 stalks celery or ¼ teaspoonful of celery salt, 1-3 teaspoonful pepper, ¼ teaspoonful mustard, a dash of cayenne pepper, 3 tablespoonfuls butter, 1½ tablespoonfuls flour, 2 hard-boiled eggs, 1 lemon, a ham bone, if you have it. Soak beans over night; in the morning drain and add cold water. Slice onion, and cook five minutes with half the butter. Add this to beans, with celery stalks broken into pieces and with the ham bone. Simmer 3 or 4 hours, add water as water boils away. Rub through a sieve, re-heat to boiling point and add seasoning well mixed. Bind with the remaining butter and flour cooked together. Cut the eggs and lemons into slices, removing seeds from lemons. Put into tureen and strain the soup over them.

Mrs. George Baxter.

CLAM CHOWDER.

One-half pound of salt pork; cut pork size dice. Put in hot kettle until grease is tried out, then put in 1 quart of hot water. Chop 6 good-sized potatoes, 4 medium-sized onions, 1 head celery, 3 dozen clams, chopped; save juice, strain, add with 2 quarts and a pint of hot water. Let this boil two hours or more; before taking off add 1 pint of milk, 6 rolled Water biscuits, put salt and pepper (some like red pepper best). You can add parsley or tomatoes, but is very good without.

Mary H. Walker.

CLAM CHOWDER.

One dozen medium-sized clams, ¼ pound of fat salt pork, 3 good-sized onions, 8 potatoes, ½ can tomatoes, ½ teaspoonful of lemon extract or lemon juice. Cut pork in dice, slice onions thin, put in stewpan and fry until brown. Add 3 pints of hot water and juice from clams. Cut potatoes in dice and put into boiling mixture; when nearly done, add the tomatoes.

Cook until potatoes are thoroughly done, then add clams, chopped fine, 1 teaspoonful salt and a dash of black pepper. Let simmer (**not boil**) for two hours.

Mrs. Sylvester B. French.

FISH

FISH CUTLETS.

Season 1 pint of any kind of cold cooked fish with salt, pepper and cayenne, and make it into a paste with a little thick cream sauce, made quite hot. Put the paste on a dish to about one-half an inch in thickness, and when it is cold form into cutlets. Roll in bread or cracker crumbs, then in egg and again into crumbs. Fry in a frying-pan of hot fat until brown.

" Oscar," of the Waldorf.

LOBSTER CUTLETS.

Two cups lobster chopped fine; 2 tablespoonfuls parsley, chopped fine; salt and red pepper to taste. Put into a sauce-pan 1 good tablespoonful of butter, add to it 2 tablespoonfuls flour; add to that 1 pint of sweet milk. When cooked to a thick cream, add the lobster; mix it well. Put on a platter to cool. Shape, then roll in flour; then dip in egg, then in bread crumbs. Fry in deep fat. Serve with tartar sauce.

Mrs. P. H. Walzer.

LOBSTER CUTLETS.

Two large cups of picked lobster, 2 tablespoonfuls chopped parsley, 2 tablespoonfuls lemon juice, about 2 dashes of red pepper, a large pinch of salt. After this is prepared, mix 2 tablespoonfuls of flour, 1 cup of cream and milk, yolks of two eggs; while creamy, add to lobster, mix well and put out in little mounds to cool.

Mrs. Harry H. Ford.

STEAMED SALMON.

One cup bread crumbs, 2 tablespoonfuls butter, 2 eggs, beaten; soften with water or sweet milk; 1 can salmon, little salt and paper. Place in covered pail or can in boiling water and let steam for ¾ of an hour.

Mrs. F. E. Doolittle.

LOBSTER A LA NEWBURG.

Three hard-boiled eggs, ½ pint cream, 2 tablespoonfuls of flour, 4 tablespoonfuls of sherry, 4 tablespoonfuls of butter. Break the meat into medium-sized pieces. Mash fine the yolks of the eggs and add to them gradually 2 tablespoonfuls of the cream. Put the butter into the chafing dish and add the flour gradually. Pour in the balance of the cream. Stir until it thickens, then stir in the yolks and add the lobster meat and whites of the eggs sliced. Before serving, add red pepper, salt and the sherry.

Mrs. J. E. Larkin.

SHRIMPS.

One-half pint shrimps, fresh or canned, 1 tablespoonful tomato sauce, 2 tablespoonfuls butter, 1 cup boiled rice, 1 gill of cream, ½ grated onion, salt and pepper to taste. Put butter in chafing dish when hot, stir in onion and rice, add the cream, shrimps and tomato sauce. Stir until it boils; let it simmer for five minutes.

Susan P. White.

OYSTER CROQUETTES.

Parboil and drain one pint of oysters; cut them in quarters and mix with enough cream sauce to hold them together. Season with salt and pepper. Shape, and roll in bread crumbs, then in egg, then in crumbs again, and fry in deep fat.

LITTLE PIGS IN BLANKETS.

Season large oysters with salt and pepper; wrap each oyster in a very thin slice of bacon and fasten with a wooden toothpick; heat a frying-pan and put in the little pigs. Cook just long enough to crisp the bacon; put on small pieces of buttered toast and serve immediately. The pan must be very hot before the pigs are put in, and then be careful they do not burn. Mrs. S.

TARTAR SAUCE.

Yolks of 4 eggs, even teaspoonful flour, ½ cup butter; stir these well together. Juice of ½ lemon, red pepper, 1 cup boiling water, chopped pickle. Beat with egg-beater all the while it is cooking. Instead of this, Mayonaise dressing with chopped pickles may be used.

Mrs. P. H. Walzer.

FISH SAUCE.

One large tablespoonful flour, 2 large tablespoonful butter, creamed, nearly ½ teaspoonful salt. Put on the stove to melt, then add gradually 1 cup of boiling water. Boil about 3 minutes, then add a little onion and lemon juice. Remove from the stove and beat slowly into 2 well-beaten yolks of eggs until cool; add capers and 1 hard-boiled egg chopped.

Mrs. Archibald E. Baxter.

**GREATER ELMIRA'S
"PAY - AS - YOU - GO STORE"**

The Great Atlantic & Pacific Tea Co.

117 EAST WATER ST.

8 Choice Receipts for Cooking EIDER DOWN COD

CODFISH AU GRATTIN.

Pick 2 cups of Eider Down Codfish Cake into tiny pieces. Cover with cold water and let stand 3 hours. It is better to change the water once during that time. Then drain and press out all the water. Make a cream sauce with two level tablespoonfuls of butter, 2 of flour, 1 cup of cream and 1 of milk. Add to this 2 tablespoonfuls of finely grated cheese, mix carefully and well with the fish. Put in a shallow grating dish, sprinkle the top with cheese and brown in a hot oven.

TOASTED CODFISH.

Take 1 package of Eider Down Codfish and freshen in warm water. Let it soak a day and a night, changing the water twice during that time. When freshened enough to be pleasant to the taste, set it on the stove and let the water come gradually to the scalding point. (Never boil cod that has been previously salted and dried. That makes it hard.) Place in bread toaster, when drained, and toast a delicious brown over the live coals. While still hot, have ready a gravy of sweet cream and butter, seasoned with pepper and a pinch of salt, unless the fish is decidedly salt still. Place in covered dish for table and pour over it the gravy. If cream be not obtainable, a gravy almost equal to it is made by rubbing 2 tablespoonfuls of flour smooth in half cup of cold water, pour it in a sauce-pan over fire, and add half cup of boiling water. Cook slowly, stirring constantly, then add butter the size of an egg and cup of hot milk, season.

STEWED SALT CODFISH.

Take 1 package of Eider Down Codfish and lay it in cold water for a few minutes to soften it a little, enough to make it more easily picked into small pieces. After picking into very small bits, put it over the fire in a stew-pan with cold water; let it come gradually to the scalding point, then turn off this water carefully and add a pint of milk to the fish, or more according to quantity. Set it over the fire again and let it boil slowly for 3 minutes, now add a good-sized piece of butter, a shake of pepper, and a thickening of a tablespoonful of flour in enough cold milk to make a cream. Stew five minutes longer and just before serving stir in two well-beaten eggs.

CODFISH A LA MODE.

Pick up a teacupful of Eider Down salt codfish very fine, and freshen by saturating the codfish slightly with cold water and strain through a cloth (requires no soaking). Two cups of mashed potatoes, 1 pint of milk, two well-beaten eggs, ½ cup of butter, salt and pepper; mix thoroughly and bake in an earthen baking dish from 20 to 25 minutes. Serve in the same dish.

EIDER DOWN COD CAKES.

One pint of raw potatoes, cut in pieces; 1 cup of Eider Down Cod. Boil together until potatoes are tender, then drain off the water and mash, beating well together; add 1 tablespoonful of butter, 1 egg and a little pepper. Shape into small cakes and fry in hot lard.

CREAMED COD.

Take one package of Eider Down Cod and lay it in cold water for a few minutes to soften it enough to make it more easily picked into small pieces. After picking into very small bits, cover with cold water and let stand 2 hours, then drain and press out all the water. For each cupful of fish add two of milk and a tablespoonful of butter. Let it come to a boil, then add a teaspoonful of cornstarch and one egg well beaten. Serve on toast.

SALT CODFISH, CREOLE STYLE.

(From Mrs. Rorer's New Cook Book.)

Take 1 package of boneless codfish (Eider Down), ½ cup of rice, 2 tablespoonfuls of butter, ½ can of tomatoes, 1 onion, ½ teaspoonful salt, 1 saltspoonful of pepper. Soak codfish over night in cold water. When ready to serve, put the butter and onion in a sauce-pan; cover and cook on back part of the stove until onion is soft, not brown. Drain the codfish, add it and the rice, which has been previously boiled for 20 minutes; pour over the tomatoes strained; cover sauce-pan and cook gently 20 minutes. When ready to serve add salt and pepper, push the rice aside and dish the fish first; put on top of it the rice, and pour over the sauce. This makes an economical and palatable dish for lunch.

CURRIED CODFISH.

Take 1 package of Eider Down Codfish and freshen in warm water. Let it soak 24 hours, changing the water twice during that time. When freshened enough to be pleasant to the taste, set it on the stove and let the water come gradually to the scalding point. (Never boil cod that has been previously salted and dried; that makes it hard.) Chop 2 good-sized onions very fine, and put them with 2 tablespoonfuls of butter in a sauce-pan; cover, and when soft add 1 teaspoonful of curry powder, 1 tablespoonful of flour, 1 pint of water; stir until boiling, and then add the fish. Cover and stand on the back part of the stove for 10 minutes. Add the juice of 1 lemon and season to taste. Serve in a border of carefully boiled rice.

Our valuable and useful cook book, containing **OVER 250 WAYS TO COOK AND SERVE FISH,** can be had free at your dealer's, or mailed to you direct from our office by writing to us and enclosing a two-cent stamp for postage.

SHUTE & MERCHANT,
Gloucester, Mass.

Our Products from the Sea are the Best in the World. The Best Dealers handle them.

MEATS

VEAL LOAF.

One and one-fourth pounds raw veal, ½ pound lean fresh pork, 2 slices salt pork. Grind fine and add 4 large crackers, 3 eggs, black and red pepper. Bake in a moderate oven.

Mrs. Edward P. Rapelyea.

DELMONICO CHICKEN CROQUETTE.

Two sweetbreads, boiled, 1 teacupful of boiled chicken, 1 boiled onion, chopped fine, 1 teacup of boiled bread and milk, ¼ pound of butter, melted, salt and pepper. Chop chicken and sweetbread very fine; mix all together.

Mrs. Edward Bruce Rogers.

MEAT LOAF.

Two pounds hamburg steak, ¼ pound salt pork, 2 milk crackers rolled fine, 2 eggs, ½ cup milk, 1 teaspoonful pepper, ½ teaspoonful salt, a little mixed spice.

Mrs. G. W. Buck.

SALT PORK FRITTERS.

Cut pork into thin slices, freshen and fry it. Make a batter of 1 egg, ½ pint milk, a little salt, and flour enough to make it quite stiff. Dip the pork, while hot, into the batter, and fry a light brown.

Mrs. Hosmer H. Billings.

CHICKEN PUDDING.

One pint of milk, 3 eggs, beaten separately, 1 teaspoonful salt, 2 teaspoonfuls baking powder, flour to make a stiff batter. When beaten up light, add 1 pint of cold chicken cut in small pieces. Bake 1 hour. Serve cut in squares with the chicken gravy.

Mrs. Maria H. Carroll.

CECILS.

One pint of chopped meat of any kind. Put into a saucepan, add ½ tablespoonful butter, ¼ cup milk, 2 tablespoonfuls cracker crumbs, 1 teaspoonful salt, dust of pepper, a little nutmeg, 2 eggs, 1 teaspoonful cornstarch. Stir over the fire about 10 minutes, and then turn into an earthen dish to cool. When cool, form into balls, roll them in beaten egg and cracker crumbs, and fry in boiling-hot lard. Serve with tomato sauce.

Mrs. J. D. Bisbee.

HOT VEAL LOAF.

One and one-half pounds veal, 1 pound fresh fat pork, ½ pound beef, all chopped together fine; add 1 cup grated bread crumbs, 1 teaspoonful of parsley, 1 teaspoonful of salt, pepper to taste, juice and grated rind of half a lemon, 3 eggs, well-beaten. Mix well the above ingredients, shape like a loaf of bread and cover with fine crumbs and bits of butter. Bake two hours. Do not add water for 15 minutes, then baste frequently. Make gravy with the bastings.

Mrs. George O. Baxter.

CREAMED CHICKEN.

One chicken, four sweetbreads, 1 can mushrooms. Boil chicken and sweetbreads; when cold cut as for salad. Into a sauce-pan put a quart of cream; into another, 4 large tablespoonfuls of butter and five even tablespoonfuls of flour. Stir until melted and pour on the hot cream and stir until it thickens. Flavor with grated onion, red and black pepper, and pour all the ingredients into a large baking dish. Cover with bread crumbs and bits of butter and bake 20 minutes. Chicken liquor may be used in preference to all cream.

"Snap Shots."

ARABESQUE.

Put in a bake dish alternate layers of cold roast beef, chopped, and tomatoes, fresh or canned, but seasoned well. Cover with bread crumbs and bits of butter. Bake an hour. A good way to use up the last of the roast.

Mrs. Roswell R. Moss.

ROYAL SCALLOP.

This amount makes 2 quarts: One-fourth pound lean ham, chopped fine, 12 hard-boiled eggs, chopped, 1 pint milk, 1 pint cream, ½ pound bread crumbs, pinch of red pepper; chop yolks and whites separately. Boil milk and cream with 2½ spoonfuls flour and a good-sized piece of butter. Make a smooth cream—not too thick; put, alternately, layers of ham and yolks and whites of eggs, bread crumbs and cream dressing. It must be very moist. Put bread crumbs on top and bake 25 or 30 minutes.

Mrs. McWilliams.

BEEFSTEAK PIE.

One and one-half pounds beefsteak, 1 carrot, 6 small onions, 2 stalks celery, 6 small potatoes, 1 pint mushrooms. Cut steak in small pieces, cover with boiling water; let boil slowly until it is nearly done, add carrot onions and celery, cut in small pieces, and, last, the potatoes. After the carrot, onions and celery have cooked about 10 minutes, and when done add the cayenne pepper and cloves to taste; make a rice gravy. Take off the stove and add the mushrooms. Line a baking dish with a rich paste and cut out the bottom paste, so to leave only the sides lined, then pour the ingredients in the dish and put crust on top; put in the oven and when done serve in the same dish.

Mrs. N. J. Thompson.

RAGOUT OF VEAL.

For this the remains of a cold roast may be used. Cut into inch pieces, to every pint of these allow: One-half pint of stock, 1 teaspoonful butter, 1 teaspoonful flour, 1 teaspoonful Worcester sauce, 1 teaspoonful mushroom catsup, 2 teaspoonfuls sherry, 1 teasponful onion juice, 1 blade of mace, 6 mushrooms chopped fine. Put the butter in frying pan, stir until a nice brokn, add flour and brown again, add stock, stir until it boils, add mushrooms, mace, onion juice, mushroom catsup, sauce; salt to taste; mix and add the veal. Place over a very moderate fire to simmer 15 minutes, then take from the fire, add wine (if you use it), garnish with boulettes of potatoes and serve very hot.

Mrs. E. S. Wyckoff.

VEGETABLES

ONE WAY TO COOK EGG PLANT.

Put in water and boil until soft. Peel and drain, season and mash. Make into patties and roll in egg and cracker crumbs and fry.   Mrs. H. M. Clarke.

RECEIPT FOR CORN-OYSTERS.

One pint pulp, beat separately 2 eggs, ½ teaspoonful salt, cayenne and black pepper, 2 tablespoonfuls flour. Fry in any preferred frying medium.   Mrs. J. A. Secor.

BAKED RICE.

Wash 1 cup of rice well, add to it 1 cup of strained broth, 2 cups of boiling water; cook slowly until it has taken up all the water and is soft. Pour into it a large cup of hot milk, in which has been beaten two raw eggs, 2 tablespoonfuls grated cheese and 1 tablespoonful of butter; stir well and add a heaping cup of minced ham and veal. Put into a mould, cover and bake 1 hour. To remove from mould, dip first into hot water and then cold and invert on platter.
    Mrs. Frank W. Durand.

CREAMED SPANISH ONIONS.

Peel and slice in quarter-inch slices; put on in cold, salted water, bring to boil and drain. Then put on in boiling water, cook till tender; drain, dot with bits of butter, dredge with flour, season and pour on enough milk to nearly cover. Shake, not stir more than possible, until creamy. (It takes an hour or less.)   Mrs. A. F. Werdenberg.

CORN FRITTERS.

Five large cups of grated sweet corn (2 dozen ears), 9 eggs, 5 tablespoonfuls milk (use cream if desired); beat the eggs well, add the corn by degrees, beating very hard; 1 large teaspoonful salt, 2½ large tablespoonfuls melted butter, 1½ teaspoonfuls sugar, 5 tablespoonfuls flour. Use the usual cooking spoon and tablespoon. Bake on griddle.
    Mrs. Archibald E. Baxter.

SPINACH.

Wash well and cook uncovered in boiling salted water until tender—about 20 minutes. Drain, rinse in cold water and chop fine. Cut fine a small onion, fry a golden brown in plenty of butter. Add flour, stir until cooked, then add water to make thin sauce. Season, add spinach, cook for an hour or more, stirring often, as it will easily burn. It is best to cook in granite kettle well greased in butter.
    Mrs. A. F. Werdenberg.

STUFFED PEPPERS.

Cut off the stem end and scoop out seeds and coarse veins of six green peppers. Prepare another pepper in the same way, then chop fine and mix with a small minced onion, 2 cups of chopped tomato, two tablespoonfuls of salad oil or melted butter, a teaspoonful of salt and an equal quantity of fine bread crumbs. Put this mixture in the peppers and replace covers. Put them in a baking-pan with a little water or stock and bake in a hot oven for half an hour, basting frequently with butter or oil. Serve hot as a vegetable. Minced chicken may be used if desired.

Mrs. Ella A. Up de Graff.

CREAMED CABBAGE.

Boil a fine, white cabbage 15 minutes, changing water for more from teakettle. When tender, drain and cool. Chop fine, add 2 beaten eggs, 1 tablespoonful butter, 3 tablespoonfuls rich milk or cream, pepper and salt to taste. Bake in pudding dish until brown. Serve hot. "Snap Shots."

SCALLOPED TOMATOES.

One quart of chopped tomatoes with juice, 3 heaping tablesponfuls of butter, melted and poured over 1 pint of bread crumbs. Season liberally with salt and cayenne and stir into the tomatoes. Cover with crumbs and bits of butter and bake. Mrs. B.

WHOLE CAULIFLOWER.

Remove the outer leaves and cut off stem close to the flower. Wash thoroughly in cold water and soak in cold salted water (top downward) for one hour. Tie in cheesecloth to keep it whole and boil in slightly salted water until tender, keeping closely covered. Remove the cloth, serve in dish with flowers up with hot cream sauce.

Mrs. Carlton K. Hevener.

❡ In order to properly cook all the good things in this Cook Book—you should have some of the SPLENDID COAL sold by the.....

H. C. SPAULDING CO.

Cor. 5th and State Sts.

Either "Phone" will reach them

SALADS

The first requisite of a salad is to have it chilled just above the freezing point.

SALAD SEASONING.

In making salads, especially vegetable salads, with French dressing, they may be varied by using different seasonings, such as garlic, tomato catsup, mushroom catsup, Worcestershire sauce, soy, mint sauce, tabasco oil, capers and celery seed.

ROQUEFORT SALAD.

Put the crisp white leaves of a large head of head lettuce into the salad bowl. Add to this 3 tablespoonfuls of Roquefort cheese broken into small pieces, add a dash of cayenne and salt, and mix thoroughly with 5 full tablespoonfuls of French dressing. Mrs. Frederick Collin.

CABBAGE SALAD.

Dressing: One-half cup vinegar, 2 eggs, butter size of egg, 2 tablespoonfuls sugar. Let vinegar come to boil, then add other ingredients beaten until light; let cool and then add 1 cup of cream whipped. Slice one medium head of hard cabbage fine, then add dressing and serve.
  Mrs. Leroy Tabor.

CABBAGE SALAD.

One-half cup vinegar, ½ cup sugar (small), 1 tablespoonful mustard, 1 egg (beaten), 1 tablespoonful butter and 2 tablespoonfuls flour. Boil in double boiler until well cooked; let cool. Chop cabbage very fine, season with salt and red pepper. Before serving, add 1 pint of whipped cream to dressing. Mrs. Harry H. Ford.

POTATO SALAD.

Eight medium-sized potatoes cut into dice (which have been cooked and well seasoned), 6 cold hard-boiled eggs, 8 stalks of tender white celery cut into small pieces, 1 tea spoonful of grated onion. Mix thoroughly with Mayonnaise dressing; when cold, place on lettuce leaves and serve.
  Mrs. Edward Gordon Crowell.

OYSTER SALAD,

Which is perfectly delicious, is made by cooking oysters in as little water as is possible to use. Drain this off when they are done. Cool and pour over them a Mayonnaise dressing. If you choose, you may sprinkle over this crisp cabbage or celery chopped very fine. With turkey or game, this cannot be equalled. Mrs. Edward Gordon Crowell.

SWEETBREAD SALAD.

Boil sweetbreads until tender. When cold cut into dice. Mix with Mayonnaise dressing, place on lettuce leaves and serve. Mrs. Edward Gordon Crowell.

COOKED SALAD DRESSING.

Three tablespoonfuls melted butter, 3 tablespoonfuls vinegar. Beat the two together and add 1 small teaspoonful flour and 1 teaspoonful mustard, 1 teaspoonful salt and 1 teaspoonful sugar, rubbed smooth in a very little water. Let all these ingredients come to a boil. Then turn the hot mixture into a well-beaten egg and stir rapidly until partially cool. A little whipped cream stirred in lightly, after the dressing is cold, adds much. Mrs. Hosmer Billings.

PREPARED MUSTARD.

Three teaspoonfuls of dry mustard, 1 teaspoonful of salt, 1 tablespoonful of sugar, yolks of 3 eggs, ½ cup of vinegar. Cook until it thickens. Mrs. Helen M. Howes.

CALIFORNIA SALAD DRESSING.

One pint of vinegar, 2-3 teaspoonful salt, 3 tablespoonfuls sugar, butter size of an egg. Boil these together. Have ready 2 eggs beaten light, 1 tablespoonful of white mustard well worked with two or three of cream or water. Pour the boiling vinegar over slowly, beat well with egg beater. Nice for salmon, lettuce, etc. Mrs. E. J. Beardsley.

CABBAGE SALAD DRESSING.

One cup of milk, 1 teaspoonful mustard, 1 tablespoonful flour, ½ cup vinegar, ½ cup sugar, 2 eggs. Let milk come to a boil, then beat the eggs, flour, sugar and mustard together and stir into milk; cook until thick, remove from the stove and add vinegar. Mrs. R. H. Walker.

MAYONNAISE DRESSING.

Yolks of four eggs, 4 tablespoonfuls salad oil, 4 tablespoonfuls white wine vinegar. Beat together and cook until thick in double boiler. When cool add 4 tablespoonfuls more of oil, 1 teaspoonful of salt, 1 teaspoonful of mustard wet with a little of the vinegar. When ready to use, add ½ pint of whipped cream. Mrs. L. S. Roberts.

SOUR CREAM SALAD DRESSING.

One egg, 1 tablespoonful flour, 1 tablespoonful sugar, 1 tablespoonful salt, red pepper to taste, ½ cup warm, not hot, water, 1-3 cup scalded vinegar. Cook to a thick paste. When cool whip stiff 2 cups of sour cream and put together. Add mustard to seasoning if desired.
Mrs. Phoebe A. Mosher.

A VERY GOOD SALAD DRESSING.

One cup heavy cream, yolks of 2 eggs, ½ teaspoonful sugar, ¼ teaspoonful cayenne pepper, ¼ teaspoonful of mustard, ½ cup of vinegar, a little onion juice. Whip cream stiff, then add yolks of eggs, sugar, pepper and mustard; beat again, then beat in the vinegar gradually.
Mrs. Maria H. Carroll.

PETER PAN SALAD.

On crisp lettuce leaves shave blanched Brazil nuts. Color neufchatel cheese a light green with pistachio coloring, roll into balls the size of birds' eggs and arrange in the shaved nuts like a bird's nest. Serve with Mayonnaise dressing.
Mrs. Fred Harmon Fulton.

TOMATO AND HORSERADISH SALAD.

Peel and chill half as many large tomatoes as you have guests. Cut them in halves crosswise, set on tender lettuce leaf and garnish with the following dressing: Mix 3 tablespoonfuls of grated horseradish, 1 tablespoonful of vinegar, ½ teaspoonful of salt and a pinch of cayenne. Then add 4 tablespoonfuls of heavy cream beaten stiff. This is a sauce which can be served with a great variety of dishes; it is delicious with broiled beefsteak.

Mrs. Henry Hess Sterling.

TOMATO JELLY SALAD.

Add half a large onion sliced, 2 stalks of celery cut in pieces and 4 whole cloves to one can of tomatoes. Cook together for half an hour, then add 1-3 box of gelatine soaked in a tablespoonful of cold water and dissolved with a little of the hot tomatoe liquid. Stir, then pour into after-dinner coffee cups and chill or pour into shallow pan and cut with biscuit cutter. When ready to serve, turn the moulds on a bed of shredded lettuce and put a teaspoonful of Mayonnaise on each.

Arabella White.

BEET SALAD.

Yolks of 4 eggs, ½ cup vinegar, 1 large tablespoonful sugar, 1 large tablespoonful butter, ½ teaspoonful salt, ½ teaspoonful mustard, a little cayenne. Mix well, adding beaten yolks last. Stir with fork until hot, but do not boil. Pour over 3 boiled, chopped beets and 2 heads of celery.

Mrs. Beecher.

MANHATTAN SALAD.

Mix an equal quantity of celery and crisp, half-sour apples cut into suitable pieces with white Mayonnaise dressing. The white dressing is made by using, in making the Mayonnaise, lemon juice instead of vinegar, and adding at the last, when the Mayonnaise is thick, whipped cream until the Mayonnaise becomes the constituency of the whipped cream. After mixing with the apples and celery, fill the shells of the apples, place upon a leaf of lettuce and garnish with sprigs of celery tops. This salad may be varied by adding to it Malaga grapes which have been blanched and seeded, or chopped nuts.

Mrs. Frederick Collin.

OYSTER SALAD.

Twenty-five oysters, 2 tablespoonfulls of tarragon vinegar 1 saltspoonful of paprika, ½ cup Mayonnaise dressing, 1 head of lettuce, 1 pint of cut celery, 1 clove of garlic, 1 tablespoonful of chopped parsley. Select small, plump oysters. Drain, wash and throw them into a kettle, bring to a boiling point in their liquor, then drain perfectly dry. (The liquor may be saved for soup.) Sprinkle the oysters with the vinegar and paprika; stand them on the ice to cool. Cut the celery into small pieces, wash and dry. Make the Mayonnaise and stand it aside. When ready to serve, rub the serving platter thoroughly with the garlic, line the edge with the crisp lettuce leaves. Arrange the oysters in the center of platter with the celery around and over them, cover with the Mayonnaise, dust thickly with chopped parsley and serve.

Mrs. Frederick Collin.

CHICKEN SALAD DRESSING.

One cup flour, ½ cup butter mixed to a cream, add boiling water until thick, yolks of 4 eggs, 1 at a time, pinch of red pepper, 1 teasponful sugar, 1 teaspoonful mustard, 3 tablespoonfuls vinegar. When cold, add juice of 3 lemons and the whites of 4 eggs beaten stiff.

MAYONNAISE DRESSING.

Put the uncooked yolk of an egg into a cold bowl, beat it with an egg beater, then add 2 saltspoonfuls of salt and 1 saltspoonful of mustard; work them well a minute before adding the oil, then mix in a little good oil, which must be poured in very slowly a few drops at a time; at first alternate with a few drops of vinegar in proportion; as the oil is used the dressing should gain consistency. When it begins to have the appearance of jelly, alternate a few drops of lemon juice with the oil, a very little cayenne pepper, then, at last, add the white of 1 egg beaten very stiff.

Mrs. L. C. Gridley.

Stewart Bros. Co.,

GOODS AND PREMIUMS.

Over 500 articles to choose from. Save middlemen's profit by dealing direct.

Factory to Home saves 50 per cent.

¶ This useful article retails for $10 anywhere. We give $10 worth of our products, and a $10 premium all for $10.

This Stove $10.00
Products.. $10.00
Total. ... $20.00
All for $10

BREADS

BOSTON BROWN BREAD.

One cup rye meal, 1 cup granulated cornmeal, 1 cup graham flour, ¾ tablespoonful soda, 1 teaspoonful salt, ¾ cup molasses, 2 cups sour milk or 1¾ cup sweet milk or water. Mix and sift dry ingredients, add molasses and milk. Steam in well buttered tins three and one-half hours.
Mrs. T. W. Elmore.

CORN BREAD.

One pint of sweet milk scalded, butter size of an egg, 3 eggs, beaten separately, ½ pint of cornmeal, ½ cup of sugar, pinch of salt. Sprinkle cornmeal into the milk, remove from the fire, add butter and salt while the milk is hot, beat the yolks and mix into the meal, add last whites beaten to stiff froth. Have ready heated hot gem pans; butter these thoroughly. Bake 20 minutes or more, according to size of pan, in quick oven.
Mrs. S. T. Benjamin.

PARKER HOUSE ROLLS.

One and one-half cups sweet milk, scalded; 1½ cups flour, stir in the hot milk; 1 teaspoonful of salt, 1 tablespoonful of sugar. When cold add 1 compressed yeast cake in ½ cup of warm water. When light add 2 eggs, 4 tablespoonfuls melted butter, flour enough to knead. When light again, roll into ½ inch thickness, spread with butter and fold together, cut in squares; raise again. Bake in a moderate oven.
Mrs. William G. Strait.

CALIFORNIA BUNS.

One large cup squash mashed very fine, 1 pint sweet milk, 1 tablespoonful sugar, butter and lard the size of an egg, a little salt, ½ yeast cake; make in a soft sponge and let stand over night in warm place; in the morning knead it stiff and let raise. When light, make into biscuits and let raise again and bake.
Mrs. Kate A. Adams.

QUICK ROLLS.

One pint of milk, scalded, 1 tablespoonful butter, melted (cool), 1 teaspoonful salt, 1 tablespoonful sugar, 3 yeast cakes dissolved in ½ cup lukewarm water; add flour for soft dough and knead ½ hour. Make into rolls and let raise 45 minutes.
Mrs. Eastman.

CORN MUFFINS.

One-half cup shortening, ½ butter and ½ lard; ½ cup sugar, 1 cup sweet milk, ½ cup cornmeal, 3 cups wheat flour (scant), 2 eggs, 2 teaspoonfuls baking powder and 1 teaspoonful salt.
Mrs. Sanford D. Haynes.

YELLOW CORNMEAL MUFFINS.

One and one-half cup meal, first cup heaping, 1½ cup flour, 2 cups sweet milk, ½ cup brown sugar, 2 eggs beaten very light with sugar beaten in, 3 teaspoonfuls baking powder in flour and meal, 1 teaspoonful salt, 2 tablespoonfuls melted butter; stir thoroughly.
Mrs. James Stowell.

RICE MUFFINS.

One cup of boiled rice, 1 cup of sweet milk, 2 eggs, 5 tablespoonfuls of melted butter, 2 teaspoonfuls of baking powder. Add flour to make a batter which will drop from a spoon. Bake in hot gem irons in a quick oven.

Mrs. F. B. Darby.

BREAKFAST BREAD.

Two and one-half cups flour (even the cups), 1 small cup milk, 2½ tablespoonfuls melted butter, 2 eggs, small half cup sugar, 2 teaspoonfuls of baking powder. Put sugar and eggs together, then add milk, baking powder in flour, butter last; bake in square tin from 20 minutes to half an hour.

Mary H. Walker.

HUCKLEBERRY BREAD.

One cup sugar, 1½ cup of milk, 2 eggs, butter size of an egg, 1 quart flour, 3 teaspoonfuls baking powder, 1 cup huckleberries. Bake in square tin. Eat hot.

Mary H. Walker.

"JOHNNY" CAKE.

One egg, ¼ cup of butter, 2 tablespoonfuls sugar, 1 coffee cup of milk, ½ coffee cup of cornmeal, 1 heaping cup of flour, 1 heaping teaspoonful of baking powder. Bake in quick oven.

Mrs. E. J. Beardsley.

....USE....

"Best of All"

FLOUR

—It makes MORE and BETTER Bread than any other known to this market.

SOLD ONLY BY

H. S. Patterson

Both 'Phones   300-2 So. Main St.

SPIDER CAKE.

One and two-thirds cups Indian meal, 1-3 cup flour, 2 eggs, 1 cup sour milk, 1 teaspoonful soda, 1 cup sweet milk, ¼ cup flour, and a little salt. When mixed, pour into a spider, made hot and containing butter half the size of an egg, melted. Then pour over the top a cup of sour milk. Do not stir this in. Bake 25 minutes. Mrs. Hosmer Billings.

SWEET BISCUITS.

Make a good baking powder biscuit, roll about ¾ inch thick. Have ready butter and sugar creamed together, spread evenly over the biscuit, and roll as you would jelly roll cake. Cut the roll into biscuits the desired thickness, place on tins and bake at once. Mrs. A. V. Carter.

INDIAN MEAL GEMS.

One-half cup sugar, 1 tablespoonful of butter rubbed into sugar, 1 cup milk, 1 egg, 1 teaspoonful baking powder, ½ teaspoonful salt, ¾ cup of Indian meal, 1 cup wheat flour. Bake in hot oven 15 minutes for gems, or 25 minutes for cake.
Mrs. Newton Benjamin.

DR. RACHEL B. GLEASON'S FAVORITE GEM RECIPE.

One quart sweet milk, 1 quart graham flour, 4 eggs, well beaten, a little salt. Mix the milk and flour together, then add eggs and salt. Beat thoroughly 5 minutes or so. Bake in gem irons; have the irons well greased and very hot. Fill 2-3 full and bake in a hot oven. Be particular about having flour very fresh.

POP-OVERS.

One egg, well beaten, 1 cup milk, ¾ cup flour, pinch salt. Heat iron gem pans. Bake in hot oven.
Mrs. Irving D. Booth.

DEMOCRATS.

Three eggs, ½ cup butter, ½ cup of sugar, 2 cups sweet milk, 1 quart flour, 4 teaspoonfuls of baking powder. To be baked in patty pans. Serve them hot.
Mrs. Woodman Demarest.

POP-OVERS.

One heaping cup of flour, 2 eggs, 1¼ cup of milk. Beat together well. Have oven hot and tins well heated.
Mrs. Edward Bruce Rogers.

BROWN BREAD.

One cup sweet milk, 1 cup cold water, 3 tablespoonfuls brown sugar, pinch of salt, 1 cup white flour, 2 teaspoonfuls baking powder, 2 cups graham flour; sift baking powder in cup of white flour. Bake 45 minutes in slow oven.
Mrs. Dumar.

DATE BROWN BREAD.

Two cups sour milk or cream, 1 1-3 cups wheat flour, 2½ cups graham flour, 3 tablespoonfuls cornmeal, ½ cup molasses, 2 teaspoonfuls soda, ½ teaspoonful salt, ½ pound dates, washed and pitted. Dissolve soda in a little hot water and add to the milk, then add molasses and stir in gradually the

dry ingredients mixed together. Fill Boston brown bread tins 2-3 full, alternating a layer of the batter with a layer of dates, and steam from 2½ to 3 hours.
Mrs. H. M. Beardsley.

WHOLE WHEAT BREAD.

Set sponge at noon of 1 pint potato-water, salt sugar (1 tablespoonful of each), yeastcake and ½ tablespoonful lard or cottolene. At bedtime, knead into sponge 3 pints of sifted flour; let raise over night; knead into three loaves, raise and bake in moderately hot oven 1¼ hours. Whole wheat bread must be baked longer than white bread.
Roosa.

WHOLE WHEAT GEMS.

Two eggs, 1 pint of flour, 1 pint of milk, ½ teaspoonful salt, 2 teaspoonfuls baking powder. Beat the eggs until light. Add the milk and salt to it, and beat the flour gradually into it. Bake ½ hour in hot gem tins.
Mrs. John B. Stanchfield.

WHOLE WHEAT GEMS.

One egg, piece of butter size of hickorynut (melted), 2 tablespoonfuls of sugar, 1 cup milk, 3 teaspoonfuls baking powder, 2 cups whole wheat flour.
Mrs. C. S. Jones.

WHOLE WHEAT PANCAKES.

One cup fresh buttermilk or sour cream, pinch salt; mix with whole wheat flour until very stiff; ½ teaspoonful soda mixed with ¼ cup boiling water stirred into batter while foaming. Bake on moderately hot griddle, as cakes will be sticky if griddle is too hot or milk too sour.
Roosa.

QUICK WAFFLES.

One pint of milk, 3 cups flour, 1 teaspoonful salt, 1 teaspoonful butter, 2 heaping teaspoonfulls of baking powder, 3 eggs. Beat the yolks of eggs until light, then add milk, flour and salt. Give the whole a good beating, add butter, melted, and, last, the whites of the eggs beaten stiff and the baking powder. Mix thoroughly and bake.
Mrs. E. L. Wyckoff.

Good Eaters

¶ If you are fond of the BEST Home-made Baking—try my Cream Rolls, Fried Cakes, Cookies and all kinds of Fancy Cakes : : : :

Mrs. Jay S. Bodle

501 Baldwin St.   Elmira, N. Y.

WAFFLES.

One-half cup butter beaten to a cream, 4 yolks of eggs beaten and added to butter, ½ pint milk, ½ pint cream, 1 pint flour, salt; add the beaten whites last.

Mrs. W. I. Booth.

BISCUIT TORTONI.

Beat yolks of 6 eggs with small ½ cup of powdered sugar, a small ½ cup of Maraschino and ¼ cup Swiss Kirch. Beat well, put in a basin of hot water and cook for 5 minutes, beating all the time. Remove from fire and place in a pan of ice water to cool. Then add a pint of whipped cream, sweetened and flavored with vanilla. Put in paper cases and sprinkle powdered macaroons over them. Place on ice and chill for 2 hours.

Mrs. C. E. Rapelyea.

PUDDINGS

GRAHAM PUDDING.

One small cup butter, 1 cup sugar, 1 cup molasses, 1 cup sweet milk, 1 cup raisins, 1 egg, ¼ cup citron, 1 teaspoonful soda, 1 teaspoonful cinnamon, 1 teaspoonful cloves, 1 teaspoonful nutmeg, cups graham flour. Steam 2½ hours.

Mrs. Harry H. Ford.

ENGLISH PLUM PUDDING.

Two cups of suet chopped very fine, 2 eggs well beaten, 2-3 of a cup of sweet milk, 2 cups of seeded raisins, 1 cup of best English currants, ¼ cup of chopped citron, teaspoonful of salt, ½ a grated nutmeg, teaspoonful of cinnamon, flour to make a very stiff batter. Boil in a tightly covered mold 4 or 5 hours. Serve hot with hard or brandy sauce.

Mrs. Lewis C. Gates.

BLACK PUDDING.

One egg, 1 cup molasses, 1 cup raisins, chopped, seeded and floured, 1 teaspoonful soda, ¼ teaspoonful salt, 1 cup warm water, spices to taste; flour enough to make a batter as stiff as an ordinary cake. Steam 2½ hours.

Mrs. Hosmer Billings.

M. B. THOMPSON

Dealer in

Fine Groceries

York State 'Phone 522

214 W. Water St.,   Elmira, N. Y.

SUET PUDDING.

Two cups milk, 1 cup molasses, 1 cup suet, 1 cup chopped raisins, 1 teaspoonful soda, 2 teaspoonfuls cream-tartar, flour to make as stiff as fruit cake; add spices, cinnamon, cloves and nutmeg, to taste. Boil 3 hours in a tin mold; one with a tube in center is best. Must not allow water to stop boiling, but fill up the kettle occasionally with boiling water. Sauce: Beat together 1 cup sugar, ½ cup butter, 1 large tablespoonful of brandy, until light. Thicken 2 cups boiling water with 2 teaspoonfuls flour. Just before serving stir the two together. Mrs. Irving D. Booth.

SUET PUDDING.

One cup each of chopped suet, molasses, milk and chopped raisins, ½ cup each of English currants and sliced citron. Stir in flour until thick as pound cake. Steam 3 hours. Sauce: Cream 1 cup sugar and ½ cup butter, add 1 tablespoonful flour, after which add 1 cup boiling water, letting it boil 5 minutes; beat the yolk of 1 egg and add while hot, stirring briskly. When cold add the white of 1 egg beaten lightly, flavor with sherry or brandy. Mrs. Frank Darby.

SPONGE PUDDING.

One-fourth cup sugar, ¼ cup butter, ½ cup flour, 5 eggs, 1 pint milk, boiled; mix sugar and flour wet with little cold milk and stir into the boiling milk. Cook until thick and smooth, add butter, and when well mixed stir in the well-beaten yolks of the eggs, then add the whites beaten stiff. Bake in cups or shallow pudding dish. Place the dish in pan of hot water while in oven. Three-fourths of an hour to make and bake. Serve with cream sauce. Sauce: One-half cup butter, 1 cup powdered sugar, wine or vanilla to flavor. Beat butter to cream, add sugar gradually, then flavoring, and milk or cream; when all is beaten enough to be smooth, place bowl in basin of hot water and stir till smooth and creamy. Takes only a few moments to prepare. Mrs. David C. Robinson.

CRANBERRY SHORTCAKE.

One quart cranberries, 1 pint water, 1 pint sugar. Boil until tender, strain, reserve thick part for cake and juice for sauce. One pint flour, 1 tablespoonful butter, 4 teaspoonfuls baking powder, ½ teaspoonful salt, 1 cup milk. Sift salt, flour and baking powder together, rub in butter, add milk to make soft dough. Divide in two parts, put one part in bottom of dish, add cranberries, then the other part. Bake and pour sauce over, to which you have added 1 tablespoonful of butter. Mrs. Eastman.

PUFF PUDDING.

One quart milk, 4 eggs; separate the eggs, beat in the yolks; 4 tablespoonfuls sugar, 1 tablespoonful flour, boil the milk and stir in the yolks, then add ½ cup of cocoanut; beat the whites very stiff, add 5 tablespoonfuls sugar, beat the whites and sugar well and drop from a tablespoon over the custard. Flavor the custard to taste, place in the oven to brown very light. Mrs. L. C. Gridley.

JELLIES WITH EXTRACTS

LEMON JELLY.
Soak a package of Plymouth Rock Gelatine in 1 pint of cold water 30 minutes; then add 2 pints of hot water, 1½ cups of sugar (or sweeten to taste), 2 teaspoonfuls lemon extract and stir until sugar is dissolved. Set on ice to harden and let it remain on ice until ready to serve.

ORANGE JELLY.
Soak a package of Plymouth Rock Pink Gelatine in 1 pint of cold water 30 minutes; add 2 pints of hot water, 1½ cups of sugar, flavor with orange extract, and stir until sugar is dissolved. Set on ice until wanted to serve.

In a similar manner other jellies may be made, using extracts of raspberry, pineapple, strawberry, etc.

In serving these jellies cut across and across, breaking it up into crystals and placing it lightly in glass dishes. Eat plain or with cream and sugar; delicious with whipped cream.

WINE JELLY.
Soak a package of Plymouth Rock Gelatine in one pint of cold water 30 minutes; then add 1½ pints of hot water. Stir until gelatine dissolves and then add ½ pint of wine, 1½ cups of sugar, stir until sugar dissolves. Keep on ice to harden and until wanted to serve. If more wine is desired use less hot water. Excellent with Pink Gelatine.

PINEAPPLE JELLY WITH FRESH FRUIT.
Take a pint or more of fresh grated pineapple, add hot water to make up a quart, add 1½ cups of sugar and boil 10 or 15 minutes. Meanwhile soak a package of Plymouth Rock Gelatine in a pint of cold water 30 minutes or more; then add the quart of hot mixed fruit and juice and stir in gently until the gelatine is dissolved. Set on ice to harden and until wanted to serve. Large fruit like canned apricots, peaches, etc., may be cut in halves or quarters and used as in the above recipe.

JELLIES WITH RIPE, FRESH FRUIT.
Pare and quarter or slice half a dozen or more ripe peaches, or other soft fruit, sprinkle with sugar and set one side. Soak a package of Plymouth Rock Gelatine in 1 pint of cold water 30 minutes; add 1½ pints of hot water to dissolve it, then add 1½ cups of sugar, and lastly the fruit. Set on ice to harden and until ready to serve. Whole raspberries and strawberries are very nice this way.

SNOW PUDDING.
Soak a package of Plymouth Rock Gelatine in 1 pint of cold water 30 minutes; add 1½ pints hot water to dissolve; 1½ cups of sugar and 2 teaspoonfuls of lemon or other flavoring extracts. Stir until sugar is dissolved; pour into a very shallow dish and set on ice until it slightly jells or thickens; beat to a stiff froth the whites of three eggs and a pinch of salt, beat in the gelatine until light and frothy and set back on ice until ready to serve. Sauce: Beat the yolks of the eggs with a cup of sugar and two teaspoonfuls of cornstarch. Scald 1 quart of milk and turn it into the yolks, heat until it thickens, stirring all the time; add vanilla and a pinch of salt and let it cool. Using a little wine or brandy in the Snow Pudding makes Princess Pudding.

 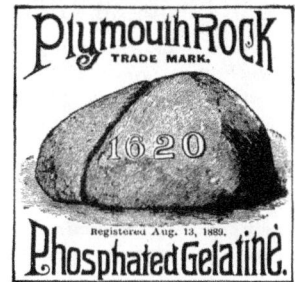

PRUNE PUDDING.

Soak 1 pound of prunes over night, remove the stones and cook till tender, add 1 cup of sugar and when cool press through a colander. Beat the whites of 3 eggs stiff and add to the prunes. Have ½ box of gelatine soaked ½ hour in cold water, then put on the fire until dissolved, and stir into the prunes and eggs. Turn into a mold. Serve cold with a custard or whipped cream.

Harriet L. Gates.

CHARLOTTE RUSSE.

One ounce of gelatine (Cox's preferred) dissolved in one pint of milk, let stand in warm place until dissolved, sweeten, flavor and strain. Have ready 1 quart of sweet cream whipped to a froth; pour the gelatine and milk into the cream, stirring well. As soon as cold, have ready a mold, rubbing the white of an egg around it and lining it with split lady-fingers, wet also with the white of egg. Let stand in ice box over night is best.

Mary H. Walker.

STRAWBERRY PUDDING.

One pint of rich milk, 2 tablespoonfuls of cornstarch, a scant half-cupful of sugar, whites of 3 eggs, a little salt, 1 teaspoonful vanilla. Beat whites of eggs to a stiff broth. Dissolve the cornstarch in a little of the milk. Stir the sugar into the remainder of the milk and place on fire in double boiler. When scalding hot, stir in dissolved cornstarch and stir constantly until it becomes a smooth paste. Cook about 10 minutes. Take from the fire and stir in lightly the beaten whites and pour into mold to cool.

Arabella White.

SUET PUDDING.

One cupful of suet, 1 cup molasses, 1 cup sour milk, 1 cup raisins, 1 cup currants, a little citron, 1 teaspoonful of soda, 1 teaspoonful of salt, 3 cups of flour, 1 teaspoonful cinnamon, ½ teaspoonful cloves, ½ of a nutmeg. Steam 3 hours. Serve with wine sauce.

Mrs. S.

ENGLISH PLUM PUDDING.

Two pounds currants, 1 pound seeded raisins, 1 pound beef suet chopped fine, 1 pound brown sugar, ¾ pound flour, 2 tablespoonfuls bread crumbs, 1 tablespoonful ground ginger, 2 teaspoonfuls cinnamon, 2 teaspoonfuls allspice, 1 teaspoonful nutmeg, grated, ¼ pound citron, cut fine, ¼ pound candied lemon peel. Wet the mixture with 8 well-beaten eggs, stirring until thoroughly mixed. Butter a strong cloth, tie very tight and boil 12 hours.

Mary A. Andrews.

STEAMED BREAD PUDDING.

Two cups fine bread crumbs, ½ cup chopped suet, ½ cup molasses, 1 cup sweet milk, 1 cup chopped raisins, 1 egg, ½ teaspoonful soda in milk, ½ teaspoonful cloves and cinnamon, pinch of salt. Cover closely and steam 2 hours. Serve with any good sauce.

Mrs. Fred A. Hudson.

RICE PUDDING.

One-half cup of rice, 1 quart of rich milk. Cook well for about 3 hours; when cold, stir in 1 cup of sugar, 1 teaspoonful of vanilla. Let stand until time to use, then stir in ½ pint of whipped cream.

Mrs. Ferdinand V. Wyckoff.

STRAWBERRY PUDDING.

One cup of sugar, 2 tablespoonfuls melted butter, 2 eggs, 1 cup milk, 2 cups flour, 1 teaspoonful soda, 2 teaspoonfuls cream of tartar. Steam 1 hour. Sauce: One cup of sugar, ½ cup of butter, cream together; whites of 2 eggs, beaten; 2 cups of mashed strawberries.   Mrs. G. W. Buck.

DANDY JACK.

One quart sweet milk, yolks of 4 eggs, 5 tablespoonfuls of sugar, 2 tablespoonfuls of cornstarch. Bring the flavored milk to boiling and add the sugar and cornstarch and yolks of the eggs, which have been thoroughly beaten. Let this boil until rather thick; when cooled, pour into a baking dish and cover with the whites of eggs beaten to a stiff froth with 4 small tablespoonfuls of sugar. Brown in quick oven and serve cold with hot chocolate sauce or hot maple syrup.
   Mrs. Frank B. Darby.

MARSHMALLOW PUDDING.

Beat the whites of 4 eggs very stiff. In the meantime boil ½ cup of water with 1 tablespoonful of Hazard's O. X. gelatine, then add another ½ cup of cold water. Beat slowly into the whites of eggs, then add 1 cup granulated sugar, 1 teaspoonful flavoring; divide into three parts, add desired coloring for each part. Line a pudding dish with fine paper, add the parts and keep in ice-box for an hour or more.
   Mrs. Henry Feuchtwanger.

STEAMED CHOCOLATE PUDDING.

Three-fourths cup sugar, butter size of egg, 1 egg, ½ cup sweet milk, 1 teaspoonful baking powder, 2 squares of chocolate melted, flour as for cake (about 2 cups); steam about 2 hours, serve hot with whipped cream.
   Mary H. Walker.

SUET PUDDING.

One cup suet, chopped fine, 1 cup raisins, 3 cups flour, ½ tablespoonful salt, 1 cup molasses, 1 cup milk, 1 teaspoonful cinnamon, 1 teaspoonful baking powder. Add molasses to suet, then milk; mix well, add salt, flour and cinnamon and then flavored raisins. Turn in buttered dish and steam 3 hours. Brandy Sauce: One-fourth cup butter, 1 cup sugar, whites of 2 eggs, 1 gill boiling water, 1 gill sherry or brandy. Beat butter to a cream, then add sugar gradually; beat well, add one unbeaten egg, then the other; beat all very light. When ready to use, add brandy and boiling water. Set bowl in boiling water and stir until frothy.
   Mrs. M. M. Conklin.

CHOCOLATE CUSTARD.

One-fourth pound Baker's chocolate, 1 pint milk, ¼ pound sugar, 3 eggs. Soak the chocolate in warm water until smooth, after which mix the chocolate with the milk, sugar and eggs. Put in small forms and bake in oven until well browned, forms to be in dripper with water to steam. Put on ice and serve cold with whipped cream. Will serve 6 people.   Mrs. Edward P. Rapelyea.

RICE PUDDING WITH WHIPPED CREAM.

One cup of rice, 1 pint of cream, ½ cup of powdered sugar, ½ teaspoonful of vanilla. Boil the rice and when cooked take off stove to cool. Whip the cream and add sugar. Fold in the rice, put in glass dish and set in cool place until needed. Heap a little whipped cream around dish and serve with a custard. Mrs. N. J. Thompson.

SNOW BALL PUDDING.

Three eggs, 1 cup sugar, 1 cup sifted flour, 1½ teaspoonfuls baking powder, 3 tablespoonfuls water, grated rind and 1 tablespoonful of juice of a lemon. Beat the yolks and sugar together until light, add the water, lemon juice and rind, then the flour and beaten whites. Fill cups half full, set in steamer and steam half an hour. Sift powdered sugar over and serve with foamy sauce made with 1-3 cup butter, 1 cup powdered sugar, creamed, 1 tablespoonful cream. Put in double boiler until hot, add 1 cup whipped cream.
 Mrs. R. R. Moss.

CARAMEL PUDDING.

One-half pint of brown sugar, ½ pint of water, ¼ box of gelatine, 4 eggs, 1 teaspoonful of vanilla. Soak the gelatine in 1 gill of water for two hours. Put the sugar and other gill of water in a small sauce-pan and set on the fire. Boil until the mixture becomes a thick syrup; add gelatine and vanilla and heat again to boiling point. Beat the whites of the eggs to a stiff, dry froth; pour the hot syrup on the eggs, beating briskly all the time. Turn in a mold and serve very cold with custard sauce. Custard Sauce: Three gills of milk, 4 egg yolks, 3 tablespoonfuls of sugar, ½ teaspoonful of salt, ½ teaspoonful of vanilla. Mrs. Lora Fitch.

SPANISH CREAM.

Soak half a box of gelatine in half a tumbler of cold water 1 hour. Put 1½ pints of milk on the stove and let it come to boiling point. Have ready the yolks of 3 eggs and 1 small cup sugar well beaten. Add first the gelatine, a little at a time, then the yolks and sugar, and let all boil until it curdles or separates. Meanwhile have the whites of the eggs beaten to a stiff froth, stir in quickly and take immediately from the fire. Flavor with vanilla and lemon. Pour into a mold and set away to congeal. When ready to serve, turn out as you would jelly. Serve with sweetened cream, which should also be flavored with vanilla and lemon.
 Mrs. William H. Stowell.

SPONGE PUDDING.

One pint sweet milk, ½ cup sugar, ½ cup flour, ½ cup butter, 5 eggs. Wet the flour with part of the milk, then cook it in all the milk 10 minutes; add the butter and sugar while hot. When cool, add the yolks of 5 eggs, well beaten, then add the beaten white and stir thoroughly. Bake in a two-quart basin set in a pan of hot water half an hour. Serve with butter and sugar sauce. Adelaide P. Hall.

ITALIAN CREAM.

One cup baked apple pulp, white of two eggs, 1 cup sugar. Beat apple, eggs and sugar together a half hour; make a thin custard of the yolks of the eggs, ½ cup of sugar, 1 tablespoonful of flour or cornstarch, 1 cup of milk. Drop a spoonful of the white part in a dish and dip the custard around it.   Mrs. N. P. Bowen.

CHOCOLATE SAUCE.

One-half cake of Baker's chocolate (4 squares), 1 cup powdered sugar, ½ cup cream, 1 teaspoonful vanilla. Grate chocolate, put in sugar and let melt in double boiler. Add cream and vanilla. Cook slowly until required consistancy—about 10 minutes.   Mrs. J. D. Bisbee.

GRAPE SAUCE.

Boil grapes (blue grapes) until tender in as little water as possible. Strain; add cornstarch (about 1 dessertspoonful to a pound of grapes) dissolved in cold water; sweeten to taste. Boil 8 minutes. Serve cold with cream. The sauce should be about as thick as apple sauce.

Mrs. Merle D. Thompson.

PINEAPPLE ICE CREAM.

One quart rich cream, 1½ cups granulated sugar, 1 grated pineapple. Heat the cream in double boiler with the sugar until scalding hot. When thoroughly cold, add grated pineapple and freeze. This is the best method of making cream; it is peculiarly smooth and velvety, and it also prevents cream from turning sour.   Mrs. Edward Gordon Crowell.

AMBERG'S
ICE CREAM and ICES

❡ Our aim is to make the finest Ice Cream and Ices that can be produced. We are not satisfied to be Number 2 or 3 or 10 : : :

We can surely suit you

AMBERG, opp. Academy

MAPLE MOUSSE.

1 quart cream, yolks of 3 eggs, ¾ cup maple syrup. Mix syrup with yolks and cook in double boiler until like custard. Stir constantly. Take from fire and whip until cold; then stir in the cream, whipped stiff. Pack in salt and ice for two hours.
Mrs. Chas. S. Mather.

ALMOND-RICE PUDDING.

Blanch ½ cup sweet almonds, drain and chop fine. Put them into a double boiler with 1 pint of milk, 1 cup of clear coffee, ¼ cup of sugar and ½ teaspoonful of salt. When scalding hot, add 1 small cup of well washed rice and cook until tender. Turn into a dessert dish and place blanched or salted almonds over the surface. Serve with cream.
Mrs. Mary Agnes Whittier.

FRUIT SHERBET.

Three cups water, 3 cups sugar, 3 bananas (mashed), 3 oranges (grate the rind of 2), 3 lemons, 1 tablespoonful of gelatine soaked in a little cold water, whites of 3 eggs. Make syrup of sugar and water and add the gelatine; add the fruit to syrup and, when partly frozen, the whites of eggs. English walnuts add greatly to the sherbet.
Mrs. Evan I. Pattengill.

BISQUE ICE CREAM.

One quart fresh milk; when hot add well-beaten yolks of 5 eggs, 2 cups sugar, 1 large tablespoonful of flour. Let boil about 10 minutes, stirring constantly, let cook. Roll ½ pound stale macaroons fine. Place 1 cup of grated cocoanut (shredded will do) in the oven on a shallow tin to brown; add to the cold custard, then add 3 pints of rich cream and a good half-pint of sherry.
Mrs. Evan I. Pattengill.

PIES

PIE CRUST.

One cup lard, 2½ cups flour, ½ cup ice water, salt. Mix flour and lard thoroughly together with silver fork, then add water.
Mrs. Edward Sheives.

CHOCOLATE PIE.

Three large tablespoonfuls of grated chocolate, 1 large cup of milk, ¾ cup of sugar, 1 heaping teaspoonful of flour, 3 eggs (yolks only), flavor with vanilla, and boil. Bake the bottom crust and fill with the mixture. Make a meringue of the whites and two tablespoonfuls of granulated sugar. Spread over the top and brown.
Mrs. Edward Gordon Crowell.

LEMON PIE.

One cup milk and 1 tablespoonful of constarch put on to cook in double boiler. The yolks of 3 eggs beaten up with 1 cup of sugar, a little butter and juice and rind of 1 lemon. Add to milk and cook until stiff.
Mrs. C. E. Rapelyea.

BANANA CREAM PIE.

Bake bottom crust first, then take out of oven and slice 3 good-sized bananas on the crust, then pour over the custard and put on meringue and bake just long enough to brown meringue. Custard: Put 1 pint milk in double boiler, let come nearly to a boil, then take 2 tablespoonfuls of cornstarch dissolved in a little cold water and beat the yolks of two eggs and stir in the cornstarch. Stir this into heated milk; when it thickens, remove from fire, let cool a little, then add 1 cup sugar and 1 teaspoonful vanilla. Meringue: Beat the whites of 2 eggs, add 1 tablespoonful cold water, beat to stiff froth and add 3 tablespoonfuls of sugar and a teaspoonful of vanilla.

Mrs. Dumars.

MINCE MEAT.

Two pounds raisins, 2 pounds currants, 2 pounds suet, ½ pound citron, 5 oranges, 5 lemons, 1 peck apples, 2 pounds brown sugar, 1 pint brandy, 1 pint boiled cider, 1 tablespoonful almond extract, 1 tablespoonful mace, 1 tablespoonful cinnamon, 1 teaspoonful cloves, 1 teaspoonful ginger, 1 nutmeg. Do not cook.

Mrs. L. C. Gridley.

ORANGE PIE.

One large orange, 6 ounces sugar, 3 eggs, butter the size of an egg, 1 pint of milk, 2 crackers rolled fine. Use round crackers.

Claire M. Howes.

ORANGE PIE.

Three eggs, 1½ cups of sugar, ½ cup butter, ½ cup sweet milk, ½ teacupful cornstarch dissolved in the milk, 1½ cups flour, 1½ teaspoonfuls baking powder. Bake in two tins. Split and make into two pieces. Filling: The juice and grated rind of 2 oranges and 1 lemon, 1 cup sugar, 1 cup boiling water, 2 tablespoonfuls of flour. Mix flour and sugar and squeeze juice or oranges and lemon on them. Then add boiling water and cook about 10 minutes. Put the filling between the two pies and sprinkle powdered sugar on top.

Mrs. John B. Stanchfield.

RAISIN PIE FILLING.

One and three-fourths cups hot water, 1¼ cups sugar, 1 cup raisins, 1 tablespoonful vinegar, 1 small piece butter, pinch of salt, 1 tablesponful flour.

Mrs. William Easterbrook.

CRANBERRY PIE.

One cup cranberries, 1 cup raisins, 1 cup sugar, 1 tablespoonful flour, 1 small cup hot water, 1 teaspoonful vanilla.

Mrs. William G. Strait.

SOUR MILK PIE.

One cup of sugar, 1 tablespoonful of flour, ½ cup of chopped raisins rolled in flour, 1 cup of thick sour milk; season with nutmeg. Bake with two crusts.

Mrs. J. Maxwell Beers.

MINCE MEAT.

Two pounds of beef, roasted, 1¾ pounds of beef suet, 2 pounds of raisins, 2 pounds of currants, ½ pound of citron, 3 pounds of sugar, 1 pint brandy, 1 pint wine, allspice, cloves, cinnamon and nutmeg to taste, a little salt. Apples, 1-3 of the quantity.

Mrs. Ella A. Up de Graff.

ROYAL BAKING POWDER

will aid the cook as no other agent will to make

The dainty cake,
The white and flaky tea biscuit,
The sweet and tender hot griddle cake,
The light and delicate crust,
The finely flavored waffle and muffin,
The crisp and delicious doughnut,
The white, sweet, nutritious bread and roll,—
Delightful to the taste and always wholesome.

Royal Baking Powder is made from PURE GRAPE CREAM OF TARTAR and is absolutely free from lime, alum and ammonia.

There are many imitation baking powders, made from alum, mostly sold cheap. Avoid them, as they make the food unwholesome.

ROYAL BAKING POWDER CO., NEW YORK

CAKES AND COOKIES

CHOCOLATE CAKE.

Two cups sugar, 1 cup butter, mix to a cream; 1 cup sweet milk, 2 cups flour, 3 teaspoonfuls Royal baking powder, ½ cake Baker's chocolate, whites of 4 eggs beaten stiff and added last. Frosting: One cup sugar, 3 tablespoonfuls water, cook until it hairs; ½ cake chocolate melted or grated. Stir all into white of one egg beaten stiff.
Mrs. J. E. Larkin.

CHOCOLATE CAKE.

One cup sugar, 1 tablespoonful butter, yolk of one egg; shave ½ cup of chocolate in ½ cup boiling water, ½ teaspoonful of soda in ½ cup boiling water; 1 teaspoonful baking powder, 1½ cups flour, vanilla. Bake in two layers and use white of egg for frosting
Mrs. Sarah Cross.

DEVIL'S FOOD.

Three cups brown sugar, ½ cup butter, ½ cup hot water, 1-3 cake chocolate dissolved in part of the water, use the remaining part for 1 scant teaspoonful of soda, 2 cups flour, 2 eggs.
Mrs. Evan I. Pattengill.

CHOCOLATE CAKE.

Two cups sugar, ½ cup butter, 1 cup sweet milk, 2½ cups flour, 2 teaspoonfuls Royal baking powder, whites of 5 eggs. Chocolate Frosting: Three cups granulated sugar, ¼ cake chocolate, 1 cup boiling water, butter size of an egg. Boil until thick.
Jennie Curtis.

CHOCOLATE CAKE.

One and one-half cup sugar, ½ cup butter, ½ cup sweet milk, 4 eggs, 2 ounces chocolate, 1 heaping teaspoonful Royal baking powder, 1¾ cups flour; flavor with vanilla. Dissolve the chocolate in 5 tablespoonfuls of boiling water. Beat the butter to a cream, add gradually the sugar, beating all the while; add yolks, then the milk, then melted chocolate and flour. Beat vigorously, then add the well-beaten whites gradually, then baking powder and vanilla. Bake in moderate oven 45 minutes.
Mrs. F. E. Doolittle.

CHOCOLATE CAKE.

One-half grated chocolate, ½ sweet milk; boil together until it thickens, when cold add 1 cup granulated sugar, 1 egg, ½ cup milk, 1 teasponful soda, butter size of an egg, 1 full cup of flour.
L. A. Davis.

BLACK CHOCOLATE CAKE.

Two eggs, 2 cups sugar, ½ cup sour milk, ½ cup butter, ¼ pound grated chocolate, ½ cup of boiling water poured on chocolate, 1 spoonful soda, 2 cups flour. Measure all in one cup; stir one way.
Mrs. L. A. Davis.

HICKORY NUT CAKE.

One and one-half cups sugar, ½ cup butter, ¾ cup sweet milk, 2 whole eggs or whites of four, 2 cups flour, 3 teaspoonfuls Royal baking powder, 1 cup hickory nut meats soaked over night in milk.
Mrs. A. W. Sampson.

CHOCOLATE CAKE WITH FUDGE FROSTING.

One-half cup butter, 2 cups sugar, 2 cups flour, 3 eggs, ½ cup sour milk, ½ teaspoonful soda dissolved in the sour milk, 1-3 cake chocolate dissolved in ½ cup of hot water, pinch of salt, 1½ tablespoonfuls vanilla. Bake in two large layers. Fudge Frosting: One-half cake chocolate, 1 cup granulated sugar, ½ cup sweet milk, small piece of butter. Boil until it thickens, but do not stir.
Mrs. C. L. Stillman.

APPLESAUCE CAKE.

One and one-half cups applesauce (hot), 1 teaspoonful soda in sauce, 1½ cups sugar, ½ cup butter, ½ teaspoonful cinnamon, ½ teaspoonful cloves, 1½ cups raisins, 2 teaspoonfuls baking powder, 3 cups flour. Bake in a loaf.
Mrs. Frank Cross.

PLAIN LAYER CAKE.

One cup sugar, 2 tablespoonfuls butter, 1 cup milk, 2 cups flour, 2 teaspoonfuls baking powder.
Mrs. A. W. Sampson.

MOLASSES CAKE.

One cup molasses, ½ cup sugar, 2-3 cup hot water, 1 scant teaspoonful soda, 1 teaspoonful lemon extract, 1 teaspoonful cinnamon, whites of 2 eggs, lard size of small egg, 2 cups flour; use yolks for frosting.
Mrs. W. W. Hinman.

LADY CAKE.

Whites of 17 eggs, 1 pound sugar, ¾ pound butter, ¾ pound flour, ¼ pound of almond meats, blanched and chopped fine; flavor with almond.

BITTER BRANDY CAKE.

Two cups sugar, 1 scant cup of butter, 3 eggs, 1 cup sweet milk, 3 cups flour, 3 teasponfuls of Royal baking powder sifted in the flour; flavor with about ½ cup of brandy, or to taste.
Mrs. Johnson Beers.

BUTTERMILK CAKE.

Stir 1 cup of sugar and ½ cup of butter together until creamy, then add an egg, well-beaten, 1 cup of buttermilk in which has been dissolved an even teaspoonful of soda; put in a cup of raisins or currants which have been rolled in flour, then stir in about 2½ cups of flour; flavor with nutmeg.
Mrs. Dumas.

HICKORY NUT GEMS.

One cup of brown sugar, 1 egg, 1 cup of chopped nuts, 3 tablespoonfuls of flour, ¼ tablespoonful of soda. Place on butter paper and bake in moderate oven; it will raise and then fall, then it is done. Crease in squares. The top will have a crust, the bottom will be soft. Stick two soft parts together, making one rough square of two. Delicious and hearty.
Mrs. Johnson Beers.

GINGER CAKE.

One full cup butter, 2 eggs, 1½ cups flour, ½ cup molasses, ½ cup sugar, ½ tablespoonful ginger, 1 teaspoonful soda dissolved in a little vinegar, and then ½ cup hot water poured on it. Bake in slow oven.   Mrs. Newton Benjamin.

JESSIE CAKE.

One scant cup butter, 2 cups sugar, 1 cup sweet milk, 3 teaspoonfuls Royal baking powder, whites of 5 eggs, 2½ cups flour.   Mrs. J. Eugene Stowell.

WHITE CAKE.

Whites of 8 eggs, 1½ cups butter, 2 cups sugar, 2-3 cup sweet milk, 2½ cups flour, 1 teaspoonful cream tartar, ½ teaspoonful of soda.

JERSEY CAKE.

One pound sugar, 10 ounces butter, 6 eggs, ½ cup milk, ½ pound cornstarch, ½ pound flour, ½ teaspoonful soda, 1 teaspoonful cream tartar, 1 teaspoonful vanilla, 1¼ teaspoonful lemon. Bake in small tins; ice one-half of each cake with chocolate, one-half white icing.
   Mrs. Sibyl W. Wyckoff.

CHOCOLATE CAKE.

One cup granulated sugar, ¼ cup of butter, ¼ cup of cocoa, 3 eggs, 2 cups of flour, after sifting once, 2 teaspoonfuls of Royal baking powder; flavor with vanilla.
   Mrs. Susan B. Crane.

MOLASSES CAKE.

One cup New Orleans molasses, 1 large tablespoonful lard, pinch of salt, 1 teaspoonful cinnamon. Stir in flour just as stiff as you can stir; then put 1 teaspoonful soda in a teacup and pour boiling water on and fill cup. Pour into the above mixture and stir up good and put in slow oven.
   Mrs. Margaret Gruber.

GRATED APPLE CAKE.

One cup of A sugar, yolk of 1 egg, butter size of large egg, ½ cup of milk, 2 cups of flour, 2 teaspoonfuls of baking powder, bake in 2 layers. Filling: Two large grated apples spread upon cake, over which spread boiled iceing.
   Mrs. W. W. Hinman.

NUT CAKE.

One-half cup butter, 1 cup sugar, whites of 2 eggs, ½ cup sweet milk, 1½ cups flour, 2 teaspoonfuls Royal baking powder, 1 large cup chopped walnut meats. Ice, mark off in squares and put ½ walnut meat on each square.
   Mrs. Hosmer Billings.

HICKORY NUT CAKE.

One-half cup of butter creamed, add 1½ cups of sugar, cream together; 2-3 cup of sweet milk, 2 cups of flour, the beaten whites of 4 eggs, 1 cup of hickory nut meats cut fine, 1½ teaspoonfuls of baking powder sifted with the flour; flavor with vanilla.   Mrs. H. K. Tubbs.

LAYER FRUIT CAKE.

Two cups white sugar, 1 cup sweet milk, ¾ cup butter, 2 teaspoonfuls Royal baking powder, 1 teaspoonful vanilla, 2 cups flour, whites of 5 eggs. Bake in 2 layers. For the middle layer take 3 tablesponfuls of the white batter, ½ cup of molasses, 1 tablespoonful cinnamon, ½ teaspoonful cloves, 4 teaspoonfuls grated chocolate, ½ cup flour, 1 cup raisins, seeded and chopped, ½ cup figs, ½ teaspoonful vanilla, ½ teaspoonful baking powder. Bake in one layer.

Mrs. M. W. Darrin.

FRUIT OR COFFEE CAKE.

One and one-half cups brown sugar, 1½ cups molasses, 1½ cups butter, 1½ cups strong coffee, 1 pound raisins, ½ pound citron, ½ pound currants, coffee cup full English walnut meats, 1 teaspoonful cloves, 2 tablespoonfuls cinnamon, ½ nutmeg, 1 tablespoonful soda, 2 eggs, 7 cups flour, ½ pint brandy.

FARM CAKE.

One cup sugar, ½ cup butter, 2-3 cup sour cream, 3 eggs, scant teaspoonful soda, flavor with nutmeg, 2 cups flour.

DELICATE CAKE.

Two cups sugar and ¾ cup butter well creamed, then add 1 cup milk, 2 cups flour with 3 teaspoonfuls Royal baking powder in it, whites of 5 eggs well beaten, pinch of salt; flavor to taste and bake in 2 or 3 layers.

Mrs. J. A. Bundy.

WEDGE CAKE.

Bake a Delicate Cake in 2 layers, then put together with first a layer of boiled iceing, then a layer of grated cocoanut, then a layer of split blanched almonds, then a layer of seeded raisins, then more cocoanut, and last the iceing.

Mrs. J. A. Bundy.

MOLASSES COOKIES.

Two cups New Orleans molasses, 2 eggs, 1 cup lard, 1 cup brown sugar, 2-3 cup sour milk, 1 tablespoonful ginger, 2 teaspoonfuls soda stirred in the flour, 1 teaspoonful soda stirred in the milk. Roll out, not very thin, sprinkle granulated sugar on, then cut out and bake in quick oven.

Mrs. Margaret Gruber.

GINGER COOKIES OR DROP CAKES.

One and one-half cup molasses, ¾ cup of shortening (½ of this is butter and ½ lard), 2 eggs, 2 teaspoonfuls cinnamon, 2 teaspoonfuls ginger, 1½ teasponfuls soda dissolved in water, flour enough to drop.   Mrs. W. I. Booth.

AUNT MARTHA'S COOKIES.

One cup granulated sugar, 1 generous half cup butter, 2 eggs, 1 teaspoonful soda in enough water to dissolve it, 2 cups flour, nutmeg to flavor. Beat the sugar and butter together, add the eggs, then soda and nutmeg. Stir in one cup of the flour, turn out on the board and mix in the other cupful, saving enough of it to use in rolling. Roll rather thin and bake in hot oven.   Mrs. Sara J. Mulford.

MOLASSES COOKIES.

One cup sugar, 1 cup butter, 1½ cups molasses, 4 cups flour, 3 eggs, 2 teaspoonfuls soda, 1 teaspoonful each ginger, cinnamon and cloves. Mrs. Charles Rapelyea.

LEMON COOKIES.

Two cups sugar, 1 cup butter, 5 tablespoonfuls of sweet milk, 3 eggs, 1 small teaspoonful soda, rind and juice of 1 lemon, flour to make them soft.
Mrs. Charles S. Mather.

DROP COOKIES.

One and one-half cups sugar, 3 eggs, ½ cup shortening, 1 teaspoonful cinnamon, ¼ teaspoonful cloves, 1 teaspoonful soda dissolved in ¼ cup of sweet milk, salt, 1 cup English currants; stir stiff. Drop small pieces on buttered tin and bake. Mrs. Charles S. Jones.

GINGER SNAPS.

One cup shortening, 1 cup sugar, 1 cup molasses, 2 eggs, 1 full teaspoon soda dissolved in a little hot water with a tablespoonful of vinegar added, 1 teaspoonful ginger, 1 tablespoonful cinnamon; mix stiff and roll thin.
Mrs. W. N. Eastabrook.

EGGLESS COOKIES.

One cup shortening (butter and lard), 2 cups of sugar, 2-3 cups buttermilk, 2 level teaspoonfuls soda, nutmeg; mix quite stiff. Mrs. Edward Sheives.

MOLASSES COOKIES.

One coffee cup sugar, 1 coffee cup molasses, 1 coffee cup shortening (half butter), 3 eggs, beaten well, 1 even tablespoonful soda, 1 tablespoonful vinegar, 2 tablespoonfuls water, ginger and spice to taste; flour enough to roll well, cut out, and bake in a very quick oven to keep them soft.
Mary E. Webber.

FRUIT COOKIES.

One cup butter, 1¾ cups brown sugar, 3 eggs, 2 cups flour, 1 teaspoonful cinnamon, ½ teaspoonful cloves, ½ teaspoonful allspice, a little grated nutmeg, 1 teaspoonful soda dissolved in a little hot water, 1 tablespoonful brandy, 1 cup raisins, chopped, 1 cup English walnut meats, chopped, 1 cup currants. Alice H. Bundy.

DROP CAKES.

One cup sugar, ½ cup butter (scant), 1 egg, 2-3 cup sweet milk, 2 heaping cups of flour, 1 teaspoonful soda, 2 teaspoonfuls cream tartar. Drop in buttered tin and in center of each cake put one raisin.
Mrs. J. Eugene Stowell.

NUT WAFERS.

Two eggs, beaten well, add 1 cup brown sugar, 1 cup chopped English walnuts, pinch of salt, 3 tablespoonfuls flour, a little cinnamon. Put the batter into cooking tins, spread thinly; make in squares, puting half a walnut on each square. This makes 24. Mrs. John J. McWilliams.

ROCKS.

One and one-half cups of sugar, 1 cup of butter, 3 eggs, 3 cups of flour, 3 tablesponfuls of milk, 1 teaspoonful of soda in a little hot water, a pinch of salt, 1½ cups of raisins, chopped, 1 teaspoonful of cinnamon, part of a nutmeg, 1 pound of English walnuts (before being cracked), 1-3 as many hickory nut meats as walnut meats; blanch almonds, split and stick on top. Drop in dripping-pan (not too thick).

Mrs. Herbert C. Way.

SNOW BALLS.

Two cups of sugar, ½ cup of butter, 1 cup sweet milk, 3 cups of flour, 3 teaspoonfuls of baking powder, whites of 5 eggs. Bake in deep, square tins. The day following, cut in 2-inch squares, taking the outside off, so as to leave it all white. Take each piece on a fork and frost upon all sides and roll in freshly grated cocoanut.

Adelaide P. Hall.

GINGER COOKIES.

One cup of molasses, 1 cup of strong, boiling coffee, 1 tablespoonful of ginger, 1 cup of brown sugar, ½ cup of lard, ½ cup butter, 1 teaspoonful of cinnamon, 1 teaspoonful Royal baking powder. Mix butter and lard together. Dissolve soda in a tablespoonful of boiling water, then stir it into the molasses, which add to the butter and lard; add spices and mix well together; pour over the boiling coffee and add enough flour to make a soft dough. Then roll out about ¾ of an inch in thickness, cut with round cutter and bake in a moderately quick oven about 15 minutes.

Mrs. E. L. Wyckoff.

DOUGHNUTS.

One cup milk, 1 cup sugar, 4 cups flour, 2 tablespoonfuls melted butter, 2 eggs, salt and nutmeg, 2 teaspoonfuls Royal baking powder well sifted into flour. Stir egg and sugar and butter together, then add the rest.

Jennie Curtis.

FRIEDCAKES.

One cup mashed potatoes, 1 cup sugar, 1 cup milk, 4 cups flour, 3 teaspoonfuls baking powder, butter the size of an egg, 2 eggs, pinch of salt. Cream butter with potatoes while warm, mix with ingredients, flavor.

Mrs. Emma Carroll.

FRIEDCAKES.

Five eggs, 2 cups sugar, 2 cups milk, 3 tablespoonfuls melted butter, ¼ teaspoonful cinnamon, 3 teaspoonfuls Royal baking powder to one quart of flour; mix very soft.

Mrs. Sarah N. Murdock.

FRIEDCAKES.

Two eggs, 4 cups of flour (scant), 1 cup sugar, 1 cup milk, 2 tablespoonfuls melted butter, 3 heaping teaspoonfuls of Royal baking powder, 1 nutmeg. To fry: Have the lard sufficiently hot, so that when a piece of dough is dropped in it will immediately raise to the surface. Turn at once.

Mrs. Helen M. Howes.

FRIEDCAKES.

Two eggs and 1 cup of sugar well beaten together, 1 tablespoonful of melted butter, 1 cup of sweet milk, 3 teaspoonfuls of Royal baking powder and flour sufficient to make a soft dough; add ¼ teaspoonful of salt, 2 teaspoonfuls of vanilla.   Mrs. H. K. Tubbs.

NEW ENGLAND MOLASSES DOUGHNUTS.

One-half cup molasses, ½ cup sugar, 1 egg, 1 cup new milk, 1 heaping teaspoonful soda, ½ teaspoonful salt, ½ teaspoonful cinnamon, ½ teaspoonful ginger, ¼ teaspoonful nutmeg; flour to roll.   Mrs. Henry Terry Elmore.

FILLING FOR LAYER CAKES.

One cup sedeed raisins and 1 lemon peeled and seeded, chopped together; mix with 1 cup sugar, ½ cup cold water. Less water may be used and an orange may be used in place of lemon. This requires no cooking and may be placed on cake while warm.   Susie A. Lewis.

COCOANUT CREAM FILLING FOR CAKE.

Cream 2 tablesponfuls of cornstarch mixed with a little cold water, add 1 cup or more of boiling water, 1 cup sugar; boil until creamy, then add 1 cup of cocoanut.
   Mrs. R. H. Walker.

OATFLAKE COOKIES.

Two cups light brown sugar, 2 cups oatflake, 1 cup melted butter, ½ cup sweet milk, 1 egg, 1 teaspoonful soda, pinch of salt. Mix together, let stand 2 hours, then add 3 cups of flour. Drop from spoon on well-greased tins and bake.
   Mrs. Leroy Tabor.

BROWN SUGAR COOKIES.

One cup brown sugar, 2 tablespoonfuls of butter, 2 eggs, ½ cup of milk, 1 teaspoonful of cinnamon, 1 large teaspoonful Royal baking powder, flour enough to make a batter to drop. Bake quick.   Mrs. Susan B. Crane.

| 1780 | THE LEADER FOR 125 YEARS | 1905 |

Walter Baker & Co.'s
Chocolate and Cocoa

It is a perfect food, highly nourishing, easily digested, fitted to repair wasted strength, preserve health and prolong life.

M. BRILLAT-SAVARIN says: "Those who make constant use of chocolate are the ones who enjoy the most steady health, and are the least subject to a multitude of little ailments which destroy the comfort of life."

A new and handsomely illustrated Recipe Book sent free.

Registered U. S. Pat. Office

Walter Baker & Co. Ltd.
Established 1780.   DORCHESTER, MASS.

45 HIGHEST AWARDS IN EUROPE AND AMERICA

MISCELLANEOUS

MOCK CHERRIES.

One quart cranberries, 1 pint sugar, ¼ teaspoonful cinnamon, piece of butter size of walnut. Cook very slowly without stirring until clear.

Mrs. Eastman.

BAKED APPLES FARCED.

Pare medium-sized, solid apples, preferably a pippin, remove seeds and core. Place the apples close, but not crowded, stems down, in a granite pie tin. After stuffing with rich orange marmalade, grape fruit, tangerines, candied orange peel, cherries, nuts or dates, according to taste, pour boiling water in the tin to depth of ¼ inch. Bake on grate in oven, at first very hot, then medium heat to finish. Remove as soon as done, before they lose their shape. Serve cold, dusting with powdered sugar just before sending to the table.

Mrs. R. R. Moss.

DEVILED HAM FOR SANDWICHES.

One pound of ham (a little fat), 4 hard-boiled eggs; chop ham and whites of eggs very fine. Rub yellow to a smooth paste with melted butter. Season to taste with dry mustard, red pepper and vinegar.

Mrs. J. Maxwell Beers.

SANDWICHES.

Sweet bell peppers chopped very fine, Spanish onions, also chopped; mix with Mayonnaise dressing and spread between thin slices of bread.

A. D. M.

LUNCHEON TOAST.

Mix 2 cups of finely chopped ham with ¾ cup of grated cheese. Stir in sufficient cream to make it spread easily; add a dash of tobasco sauce, and spread thick on slices of buttered bread. Sprinkle cheese over top and brown in quick oven.

Mrs. H. M. Beardsley.

CHEESE OMELET.

Two tablespoonfuls butter, 2 tablespoonfuls flour, stir smooth in a double boiler; 2 cups milk added slowly, 1 cup grated cheese and yolks of 4 eggs, ½ teaspoonful salt and a pinch of red pepper. When cool, add the whites of eggs beaten stiff. Bake 20 minutes in hot oven.

Sibyl W. Wyckoff.

CHEESE STRAWS.

One cup flour, 1 teaspoonful baking powder, mix thoroughly; 1 cup grated cheese, butter size of an egg, a little salt and a little red pepper, enough water to moisten—about ½ cup.

Mrs. J. P. Weyer.

CHEESE WAFERS.

One-half cup grated cheese, 4 hard-boiled eggs, 1 tablespoonful French mustard, 2 tablespoonfuls butter, ½ teaspoonful salt, ¼ teaspoonful pepper. Mix in a paste and spread on crackers or for sandwiches.

Mrs. W. K. Ten Broeck.

HOT CHEESE SANDWICHES.

After cutting bread in rather thin slices, remove the crusts and spread lightly with butter, then cut thin pieces of American cheese to cover one slice of bread, season with sprinkling of mustard and cayenne pepper, cover with another slice, cut diagonally, put in hot oven. When upper side is toasted, turn them over and toast the other. Serve hot.

Mrs. J. M. Crandall.

BEAUREGARDE EGGS.

Boil 5 eggs ½ hour, cool in cold water, remove shells and chop whites fine; press the yolks through a sieve. Boil ½ pint of milk; rub together 1 tablespoonful of butter and one of flour, and add to the boiling milk. When cooked, add the chopped whites. Have ready six small slices of toast; pour over the toast ½ of the white sauce, then a layer of the grated yolks, add the remainder of the white sauce and finish with the yolks; garnish with parsley and serve.

Mrs. Mary Agnes Whittier.

OMELET.

Five eggs, the whites and yolks beaten separately; 1 tablespoonful of milk to each egg added to the yolks, with salt and pepper; then add the whites to the yolks, beat thoroughly and cook quickly in a hot pan. To be served immediately.

Mrs. Woodman Demarest.

BOSTON BAKED BEANS.

One quart Marrowfat beans, three level tablespoonfuls sugar, 3 level tablespoonfuls salt, dash of pepper, 1 pound pork chop. Wash beans thoroughly, then put on plenty of water and let come to a boil; then add 1 teaspoonful of soda and boil three miuutes and drain thoroughly. Put on boiling water and add the sugar, salt and pepper. Cover bottom of pot 2 inches deep with beans, then put in the pork and add the rest of the beans. Bake 2 days in a moderate oven.

Mrs. Carter.

UNFERMENTED GRAPE JUICE.

Pick the grapes over carefully, using only ripe and perfect ones. Crush thoroughly with the palms of hands or potato masher. Strain juice through cheesecloth bag as for jelly. Heat the strained juice just to boiling point, bottle quickly and seal, as you would canned fruit. The juice will settle as it stands, and when used can be poured carefully off the sediment.

Mrs. George Pickering.

A CUP OF CHOCOLATE.

Stir together in a sauce-pan 1 cup of grated chocolate, 2-3 cup of sugar, 1 cup of boiling water, 1 pinch of salt. When smooth, add another cup of boiling water, 1 pint of boiling milk; boil 1 minute. Dissolve 1 level teaspoonful of cornstarch in ½ cup of cold milk and stir in. Boil 1 minute longer, remove from the fire and add 1 teaspoonful of vanilla before serving. For this rule when whipped cream should be used, ½ pint of cream for a dozen cups, whipped.

Adelaide P. Hall.

GRAPE NECTAR.

Juice of two lemons, 1 orange, 1 pint grape juice, 1 small cup sugar or less, according to taste, 1 pint water. Serve ice cold. Sliced oranges, lemons and other fruit add to the appearance when served from punch bowl.

Mrs. George Pickering.

TEA PUNCH.

Make 2 quarts of tea, using 1 teaspoonful of tea to 1 quart of boiling water. Let stand 5 minutes; strain and add 2 pounds of loaf sugar. When cool, add the following fruit: 6 lemons, 4 oranges, 1 pineapple, 1 box strawberries, 2 bananas. Set away on ice for 2 or 3 hours, then strain.

Mrs. Daniel E. Rice.

RUM LEMONADE PUNCH.

Make about a quart of strong black or mixed tea. Then make a strong hot lemonade of six lemons and about 3 quarts of boiling water and sugar to taste. Let sugar and water come to a boil before adding lemon juice. Add the tea and Jamaica rum to taste. The punch may be served hot or cold.

PRESERVES

CONCORD GRAPE CONSERVE.

Three pints pulp and skins of grapes, 3 pounds sugar, 2 pounds raisins, 1 pound English walnuts broken in small pieces; cook 45 minutes.

Mrs. Maria H. Carroll.

GOLDEN CHIPS.

Six pounds of pumpkin cut in thin slices 1 inch long, 4½ pounds of light brown sugar, 6 lemons, grated rind and juice, ¼ pound of green ginger root cut fine. Put all together and let stand over night. Boil slowly 3 hours. Do not cover when boiling.

Mrs. Daniel O. Rice.

CRANBERRY CONSERVE.

Five pounds cranberries, 5 pounds sugar, ½ cup water, pulp and juice 5 oranges, 3 pounds seeded raisins. Mix well together and cook until like jam. Put in jelly jars and seal.

Sibyl W. Wyckoff.

CLIPPED PEARS.

Eight pounds pears, cut fine, 8 pounds sugar, 6 lemons, 2 ounces green ginger, 1 glass cold water. Pare ginger and cut in small bits; squeeze lemon. Cut the rind of 3 lemons in small strips and boil until tender. Boil all together until pears are clear.

Mrs. Seymour Dexter.

GRAPE BUTTER.

Take ripe grapes, squeeze pulp from skin and cook separately. Put pulp through colander to remove seeeds; after skins are tender add pulp and skins pound for pound. Spice to taste with cinnamon only.

Mrs. William H. Stowell.

PICKLES

BEET CHOWDER.

Two quarts raw cabbage, chopped fine, 2 quarts boiled beets, chopped fine, 3 cups sugar, 2 tablespoonfuls salt, ½ teaspoonful red pepper, 2 cups grated horseradish; cover with cold vinegar and keep from air.

Miss A. F. Hubbell.

RUSSIAN CHOPPED PICKLE.

One gallon cabbage, chopped, 1 gallon green tomatoes, chopped, 1 doz large onions, chopped, 2 bunches celery, cut, ½ dozen green peppers, chopped, ½ dozen little red peppers, chopped, ¼ pound white mustard seed, 1 gill salt, 2 pounds brown sugar, 1 gallon vinegar, ½ pound celery seed. Just let come to a scald and add ½ ounce of tumeric and a bottle of horseradish, and can.

Mrs. Charles Bowman.

PICKLES.

Twelve medium-sized cucumbers and 6 large onions sliced thin; sprinkle over all ½ cup salt. Let stand over night, rinse in cold water and drain. Then add ½ cup olive oil, 1-3 cup white mustard seed, 1-3 cup black mustard seed, 1 tablespoonful celery seed, 1 tablespoonful tumeric and 1 pint vinegar; can without heating.

Mrs. Sanford D. Haynes.

CUCUMBER PICKLES.

One peck cucumbers, 1 ounce cloves, 1 ounce stick cinnamon, 1 ounce whole allspice, 1 gallon vinegar, ¼ pound white mustard seed; 1 dozen small red peppers, several roots of horseradish, cut in small pieces; 1 cup salt. Put pickles in layers and spices between (glass jars are best). Put salt in vinegar and pour over boiling hot.

Mrs. J. P. Weyer.

CUCUMBER PICKLES.

One-eighth pound ground mustard, ½ pound white mustard seed, ¼ pound black mustard seed, ¼ pound white ginger root, ½ ounce red pepper, ½ ounce mace, 1 ounce whole cloves, 2 ounces allspice, 1 ounce tumeric, 2 ounces celery seed, bay leaves; 1½ gallons of vinegar, add to it 2½ pounds of brown sugar, then throw in all of the spices and mix well. Put 1 teacupful of salt to 1 gallon of boiling water and cover the cucumbers with the boiling-hot brine. Let stand in this 24 hours, then drain and rinse, throw the cucumbers in the spiced vinegar, and for 4 weeks stir up from the bottom twice a week.

Mrs. H. K. Tubbs.

CUCUMBER MANGO PICKLES.

One dozen large green cucumbers; put in medium brine for nine days. Put a weight on. Take out and slit them lengthwise; take small spoon and scoop out all seeds and pulp, rinse thoroughly. Fill the cavities with large table raisins and slices of lemon. Make a very rich syrup with cassia buds in it. Pour over boiling hot. Heat and pour over for 9 days.

Mrs. C. A. Stowe.

CUCUMBER PICKLES.

One gallon vinegar (do not heat), 2 cups brown sugar, 1 cup salt, ½ cup mustard flour; mix all together with spices and bay leaf. Wash pickles and put in crock or cans.

Mrs. M. M. Conklin.

MIXED PICKLES.

Two quarts small cucumbers; 2 quarts green, red and yellow peppers, cut in rings; 1 quart celery, cut in small pieces; 2 quarts onions, silver-skin and small; 2 quarts carrots, in slices; 2 quarts cauliflower, in pieces. Prepare in the afternoon; put a layer in a large dish and a liberal sprinkling of salt; continue in this way until all are in the dish. Put on a press and let stand over night. In the morning drain off all the water and cook each article separately; do not cook too much or they will be soft. While they are yet hot, put over the stove 1 gallon of good cider vinegar, add 4 pounds light brown sugar and 5 cents' worth of mixed spices. Let the vinegar come to a boil, put in the pickles and let them heat through, and can.

Mrs. Nelson P. Bowen.

INDIA RELISH.

Two gallons cabbage, 1 gallon green tomatoes, 1 dozen onions. Chop fine, sprinkle ½ cup salt over it and drain two hours; then add 1 ounce celery seed, 1 ounce whole black pepper, 4 ounces white mustard seed, 1½ pounds brown sugar, 1 gallon cider vinegar, boil 2 hours; 1 gill of salt, ½ teaspoonful red pepper; add ½ ounce tumeric the last thing.

Mrs. W. W. Hinman.

When you make a present of Booth's Chocolates,

you have the satisfaction of knowing you are giving the best confectionery procurable.

More care is taken and purer material is used in making **Booth's Chocolates** than any other manufacturers think necessary. Pure fruit juices only are used which gives a flavor that others are trying to imitate.

Our Fancy Packages of Assorted Chocolates are the perfection of candy making art. The dollar box is especially attractive, just the right price and contains over a pound of the most delicious confection you ever tasted.

Your dealer has constantly on hand a fresh supply of

Booth's Chocolates.

WILFRID I. BOOTH,
ELMIRA, N. Y.

More special edition reprinted books from
New York History Review

A Brief History of Chemung County, New York, 1779 -1905

Frederick Douglass' Speech at Elmira, New York 1880

Harper's New York & Erie Railroad Guide Book of 1851

The Elmira Prison Camp

Souvenir of Canandaigua, New York

Erie Railway Tourist 1874

Diary of a Tar Heel Confederate Soldier

Our Own Book : A Victorian Guide To Life

To War and Back - The Lightning Division

NewYorkHistoryReviewBookstore.com

The Park Church.

www.ingramcontent.com/pod-product-compliance
Lightning Source LLC
LaVergne TN
LVHW011430080426
835512LV00005B/374